Headfirst Into Maths

Handling Data

David Kirkby

Heinemann
LIBRARY

First published in Great Britain by Heinemann Library,
Halley Court, Jordan Hill, Oxford OX2 8EJ,
a division of Reed Educational and Professional Publishing Ltd.
Heinemann is a registered trademark of Reed Educational & Professional Publishing Limited.

OXFORD MELBOURNE AUCKLAND
JOHANNESBURG BLANTYRE GABORONE
IBADAN PORTSMOUTH NH (USA) CHICAGO

Designed by Susan Clarke
Illustrations by Charlotte Hard
Origination by Ambassador Litho Ltd
Printed by Wing King Tong in Hong Kong

03 02 01 00 99
10 9 8 7 6 5 4 3 2 1

ISBN 0 431 08021 6

British Library Cataloguing in Publication Data
Kirkby, David
Handling data. – (Head first into maths)
1.Numerical analysis – Juvenile literature
I.Title
519.5

Acknowledgements
The Publishers would like to thank the following for permission to reproduce photographs:
Action Plus Photographic, p 13 (Glyn Kirk), 26 (Mike Hewitt); Trevor Clifford, p 9; Empics
(Tony Marshall), p 21.

Our thanks to Hilary Koll and Steve Mills for their comments in the preparation of this book.

Every effort has been made to contact copyright holders of any material reproduced
in this book. Any omissions will be rectified in subsequent printings if notice is given
to the Publisher.

For more information about Heinemann Library books, or to order, please phone 01865 888055,
or send a fax to 01865 314091. You can visit our web site at www.heinemann.co.uk

Contents

Any words appearing in the text in bold, **like this**, are explained in the Glossary

Data

We often need to collect information.

We might need to collect information about traffic, or to collect votes. We might need to measure temperature, or to write scores in a game.

The different information which we collect is called **data**.

Statistics is the name for sorting the data to try and find out what it tells us.

◀ There are different ways of collecting data.

*One method is to do a **survey**.*

*For example, if you want to find out which pets are owned by your school friends, you can do a survey by asking them, and then writing their answers on a **record sheet** like this one.*

Fun to do

Find out which pets your friends have, and write the information on a record sheet.

What does it mean?

Another way of conducting a survey is to use a **questionnaire**.

A questionnaire is a set of questions on a sheet of paper. Each person who takes part in the survey has to answer the questions on their sheet. These sheets are then collected and the data is sorted. Make your own questionnaire on a sheet like this.

Do you live in Kingsway? ☐ Yes ☐ No

What is your favourite food? _____

What is your favourite drink? _____

What is your favourite colour? _____

What is your favourite crisp flavour? _____

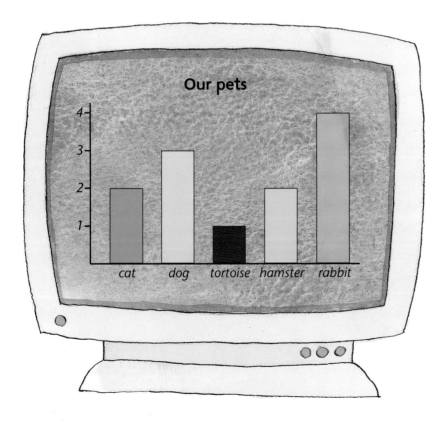

Our pets

*You can store data on a computer **database**. You collect the data, and using a computer database program, you type the information into the computer, save it, and print out a copy when you need it.*

*A **spreadsheet** is a table of data produced by a computer.*

Tallies

In the days before calculators and computers, and the days before paper and pens were used, people used **tallying** to help them know how many things they had counted.

Different methods of tallying are still used today.

▲ *One method of tallying was to carve notches in a stick. A shepherd could count his sheep into the pen by carving one notch on his stick for each sheep. When he had finished carving, he would count the number of notches to represent the number of sheep in the pen. This stick is called a tally stick.*

▶ *Another method used by shepherds was to use stones. As each sheep went into the next field, the shepherd moved one stone to his right to create a new pile. He counted the number of stones in this new pile to tell him how many sheep had been moved.*

An alternative method was to use one stone to match every 2 sheep or perhaps every 5 sheep.

What does it mean?

A **tally mark** is an easy way of counting by drawing a line.

To make the counting easier at the end, we complete a set of 5 tallies by making a 'gate', for example

At the end, we count the gates in fives.

LHI

Traffic passing the school gate in 10 minutes
bus ||||
car   LHI LHI LHI LHI ||
lorry   LHI LHI |
van   LHI ||
bicycle   LHI LHI LHI ||
motor cycle |||
other ||

◀ *This chart shows the number and type of vehicle passing the school gate. It is called a **tally chart**.*

Notice that it has a clear title.

Use your head

From the chart:
- How many vans, bicycles, cars, lorries passed the gate?
- How many more cars than lorries were there?
- How many fewer motor cycles than bicycles were there?
- How many vehicles were there altogether?

Fun to do

Do your own traffic survey. Draw a tally chart to show the results.

Pictographs

A **graph** which uses sets of the same pictures or symbols to show information is called a **pictograph** or pictogram.

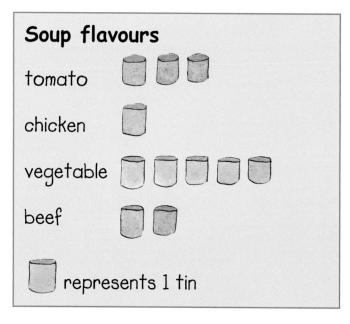

Soup flavours

tomato

chicken

vegetable

beef

represents 1 tin

◀ *This is a pictograph which shows how many tins of each flavour of soup there are.*

Notice that it is important that a pictograph has:

- *a title*
- *a chosen picture, for example, a tin*
- *the drawn tins in rows underneath each other*
- *a **key** which shows what the picture represents.*

Use your head

From the graph:

- Which flavour appears most often and which appears least often?
- How many more vegetable than beef tins are there?
- How many tins altogether?

8

▶ The pictograph shows how many slices of bread each person eats in a day.

Sometimes, if the scores are large numbers, you can make the picture stand for more than one item.

So, if represents 2 slices

 represents 1 slice.

Slices of bread we eat each day

Karen

Tom

Sanjit

Tina

Katy

represents 1 slice.

represents 2 slices

Use your head

- How many slices did Sanjit, Katy and Karen each eat?
- How many fewer slices did Karen eat than Tina?
- How many slices did all five children eat between them?

Fun to do

Collect your own data on the number of slices of bread eaten by your friends in a day, and draw a pictograph to show the results.

Frequency

The **frequency** with which something happens is a measure of how often it happens. The totals of all the **tallies** along each row in a **tally chart** are called frequencies.

▶ *Some children were asked how they liked their eggs cooked. The results were collected in a tally chart.*

How we like our eggs cooked

Boiled   HTT LHT III

Scrambled   LHT LHT LHT IIII

Fried   LHT LHT I

Poached   LHT I

These results can be drawn in a **frequency table**.

How we like our eggs cooked

Type	Frequency
Boiled	13
Scrambled	19
Fried	11
Poached	6

Use your head

- How many voted for fried eggs?
- How many did not vote for boiled?
- How many children voted altogether?

Fun to do

Roll a dice 60 times, and see how many times each of the faces are shown. Put the results in a frequency table.

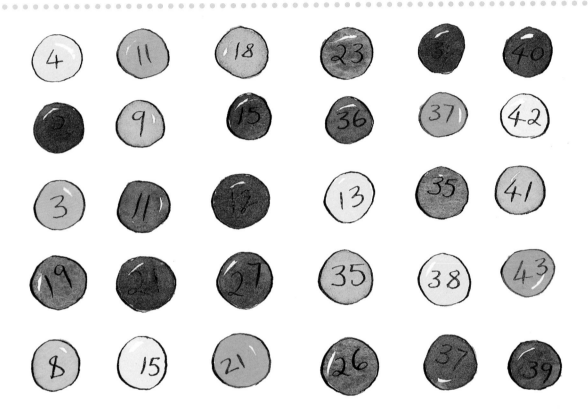

▲ These are the winning numbers in the lottery for the last five weeks.

The winning numbers can be put into groups. Those from 1 to 9, those from 10 to 19, and so on.

▶ This table shows the frequencies in each group. It is called a **grouped frequency table**.

Winning number	Frequency
1–9	5
10–19	8
20–29	5
30–39	8
40–49	4

Block graphs and bar graphs

A **graph** is a way of drawing a picture to show data more clearly.

A **block graph** draws a picture using blocks.

Each block should be the same size.

The number of blocks matches the frequency.

? Question

How many cars are there of each colour?

▶ *This is a block graph to show how many of each colour there are. Check that it is correct.*

Notice that:

- *1 block represents 1 car.*
- *The block graph has a title.*
- *The sides (or **axes**) of the graph are clearly labelled.*

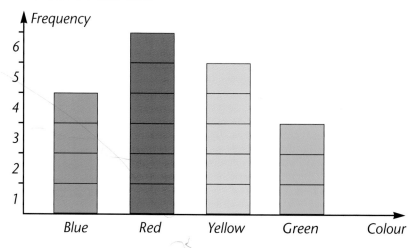

Colour of the cars

Fun to do

Take a handful of 25 different coloured cubes.
Draw a block graph to show the colours of the cubes.

What does it mean?

A **bar graph** is similar to a block graph, except that instead of drawing a column of blocks, we draw one long bar.
It is sometimes called a bar chart.

Each bar should be the same width.

The gaps between the bars should all be the same width.

The height of the bar matches the frequency.

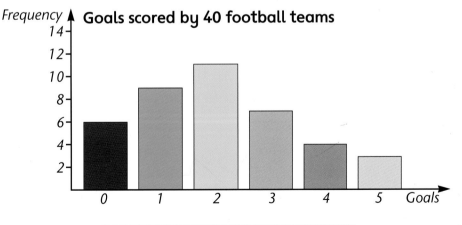

◀ *Michael Owen scoring a goal for England in the 1998 World Cup.*

▶ *Again, the bar graph has:*
- *a title*
- *one bar for each category*
- *labelled axes.*

Goals scored by 40 football teams

Frequency

Goals

Use your head

- How many teams scored 3 goals, 0 goals, 1 goal?
- How many teams scored more than 2 goals, fewer than 2 goals?

Bar-line graphs

A **bar-line graph** is similar to a **bar graph**, except that instead of drawing a vertical bar, we simply draw a **vertical line**.

The length of the line matches the frequency.

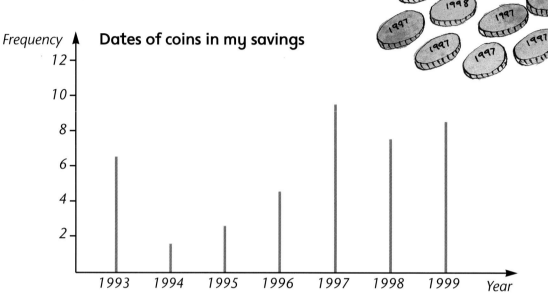

This bar-line graph shows the dates on a set of coins.

Notice that the bar-line graph has:
- a title
- labelled **axes**
- a vertical line for each category
- equal spaces between the lines.

Fun to do

Collect as many coins as you can, and sort them into piles with equal dates. Use squared paper and draw axes like those in the picture. Draw a bar-line graph to show the dates of the coins, making the lengths of the lines match the number of coins in each pile. Write about the results.

Road distances from Rome in kilometres

Town	Kilometres
Naples	192 km
Milan	487 km
Venice	395 km
Bologna	316 km
Genoa	417 km

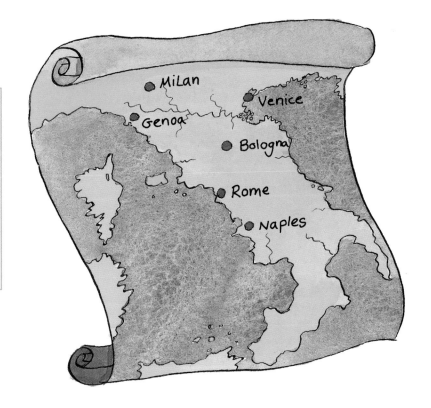

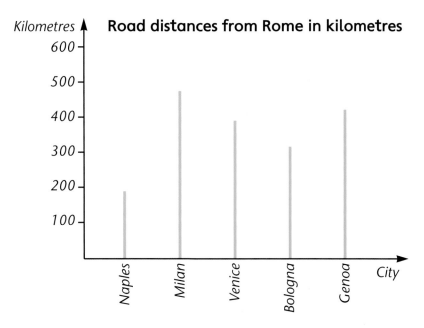

Road distances from Rome in kilometres

Use your head

From the graph:

- Which town is the furthest from Rome, nearest to Rome?

- How many towns are less than 200 kilometres from Rome?

Sorting using tables

Creating a table is one way of storing **data**.
The table is called a **database**.

Crisp flavours we like

	Name	Plain	Cheese & onion	Salt & vinegar	Beef
	Gary	✓	✓	✓	✓
	Karen	✗	✓	✓	✗
	Julie	✗	✓	✓	✓
	Sophie	✓	✗	✓	✓
	Ged	✗	✗	✓	✗
	Tiffany	✓	✗	✗	✗

▲ *The table shows lots of information clearly.*
It shows what flavours each person does and doesn't like.
It shows how many people like or dislike each flavour.

Use your head

Who:

- likes cheese and onion crisps?
- doesn't like salt and vinegar crisps?
- likes plain flavour, but not cheese and onion?

	Name	Brother	Sister	Age	Eye colour	Hair colour	Favourite colour
	Tim	1	1	9	Blue	Brown	Blue
	Pat	3	1	10	Grey	Brown	Yellow
	Greg	0	0	6	Brown	Black	Green
	Dani	2	1	8	Blue	Blond	Pink
	Sharon	1	4	7	Blue	Red	Yellow
	Amrit	2	1	9	Black	Black	Red

Personal data can be placed in a table.

This database contains lots of information.

It is easy to look at the table, and find information.

Use your head

- Who is the eldest?
- Who has four sisters?
- Who has no brothers and sisters?
- Who has a total of four brothers and sisters?
- Who has blue eyes and blond hair?
- Whose favourite colour is the same as their eye colour?

Fun to do

Collect personal data on six of your own friends, and create a database like this one. Use these headings or choose other ones. Examples of other headings are:

Favourite food

Favourite song

Favourite TV programme

House number

Shoe size

Favourite team

Sorting using charts

A **Venn diagram** is a chart which shows how numbers or objects are sorted. It uses circles inside a rectangle.

Each circle must be labelled to describe a **set**.

All numbers or objects belonging to the set are placed inside the circle.

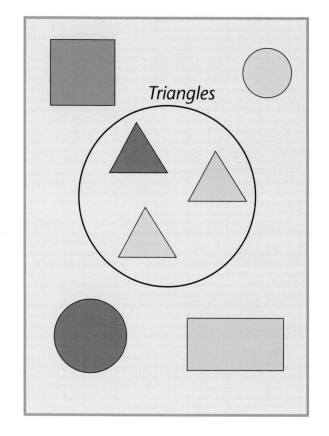

Check that the shapes are in the correct positions.

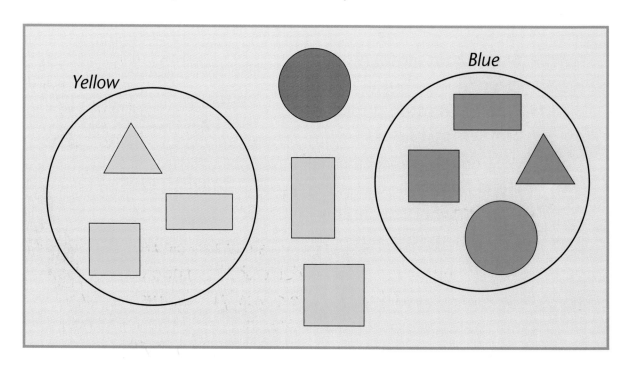

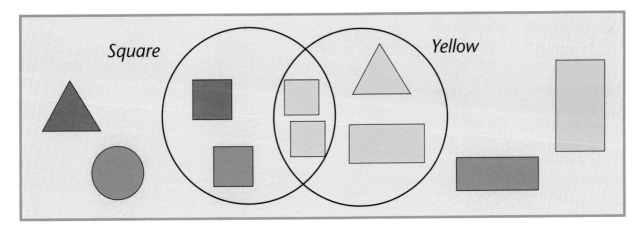

All the squares go inside the 'squares' hoop.

All the yellow shapes go inside the 'yellow' hoop.

All the shapes which are both squares and yellow (that is the yellow squares) go inside the overlap of the two hoops.

All the other shapes are placed outside both hoops.

You can use a Venn diagram to sort three sets.

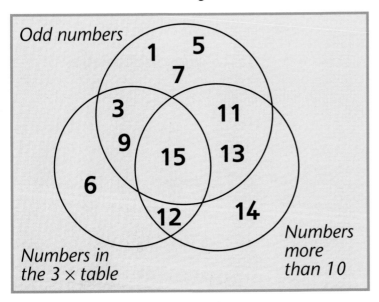

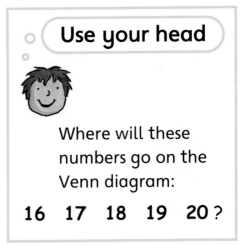

Use your head

Where will these numbers go on the Venn diagram:

16   17   18   19   20 ?

Fun to do

Draw a Venn diagram with two overlapping circles and label them 'black' and 'more than 7'. Use a shuffled pack of playing cards, and deal the first twelve cards, placing them in their correct positions on the diagram. Choose your own labels, e.g. 'red' and 'picture cards' and repeat the activity.

Reading tables

Data is often found in a table.

A table is a list or chart with either rows or columns, or both.

There are many different types of table.

One type is called a **distance table**.

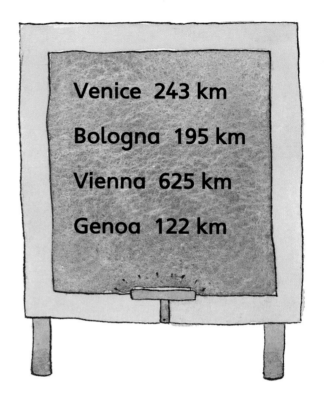

Venice 243 km

Bologna 195 km

Vienna 625 km

Genoa 122 km

▶ *To find the distance between two cities, you need to look down a column and along a row. For example, to find the distance between Bologna and Vienna, read down the Bologna column until you meet the Vienna row, and read the number 565. The distance is 565 kilometres.*

Distances between cities, in kilometres

Bologna

195	Genoa					
195	122	Milan				
497	609	677	Naples			
316	417	487	192	Rome		
126	294	243	555	395	Venice	
565	716	625	862	765	439	Vienna

Use your head

- What is the distance between Milan and Venice, and between Genoa and Rome?
- Which towns are between 400 and 450 kilometres apart?

20

▼ *This is another table with both rows and columns. It is a results table showing the scores of matches between 7 teams.*

To find the result of the Manchester United v Arsenal match, you read along the Manchester United row until you meet the Arsenal column. The score is seen as 3–2.

	Aston Villa	Arsenal	Chelsea	Everton	Liverpool	Manchester United	Newcastle United
Aston Villa	X	1–3	1–1	2–1	3–1	1–2	1–1
Arsenal	2–2	X	3–1	1–0	1–0	0–3	0–0
Chelsea	0–0	0–1	X	2–0	2–0	2–1	4–1
Everton	1–1	1–3	2–2	X	1–2	1–1	0–0
Liverpool	2–1	1–0	1–1	0–0	X	2–2	2–0
Manchester United	2–1	3–2	1–1	3–3	0–1	X	2–2
Newcastle United	1–2	2–1	1–3	2–1	1–1	0–0	X

Use your head

What were the scores in these matches:

- Aston Villa v Newcastle United
- Chelsea v Everton
- Liverpool v Arsenal?

Pie charts

A **pie chart** is a circular **graph**.

The circle or graph is divided into slices.

The size of each slice matches the frequencies.

▲ *12 children voted for their favourite sports.*
The circle has been split into 12 equal parts.
The size of each slice matches the number of votes.

▶ *Some children were asked for their favourite comic. This pie chart shows their answers.*

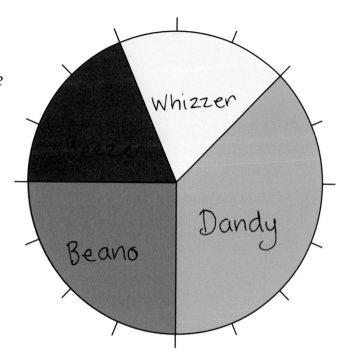

Use your head

From the graph, which comic is the most popular?

Which two comics had equal votes?

32 children took part in the survey.

Note that the circle is divided into 16 equal parts.

So, each part is worth 2 votes.

We can tell that the number of votes is:

Comic	Votes
Beezer	6
Whizzer	6
Dandy	12
Beano	8

Line graphs

A **line graph** is a series of straight lines drawn by joining points.

A temperature graph is a type of line graph.

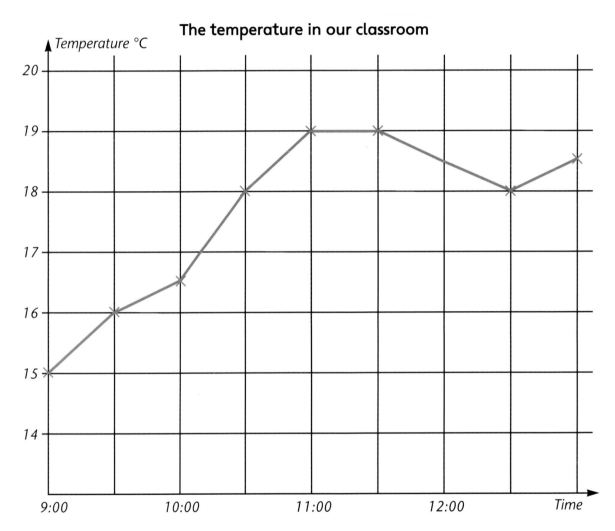

The temperature in our classroom

▲ *Notice that the line graph:*
- *has a title*
- *has time along the horizontal* **axis**
- *is joined by straight lines.*

Use your head

- Estimate the temperature at 9:45 and at 11:15.
- Estimate the time when the temperature is 17°.

What does it mean?

Another type of line graph is a **conversion graph**.

This is one straight line.

It is used to convert from one unit to another.

Conversion graphs are used to convert, for example:

• British pounds to American dollars

• centimetres to inches

• miles to kilometres

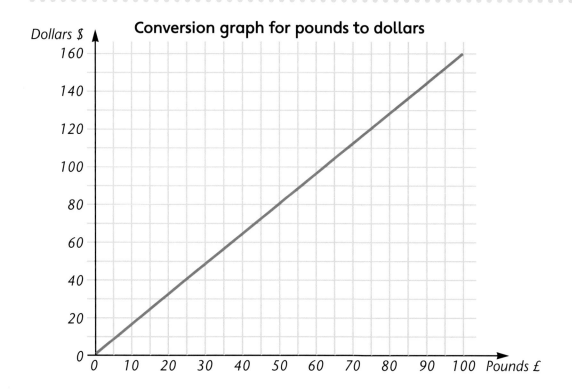

Conversion graph for pounds to dollars

Dollars $

Pounds £

🔺 *To convert £60, for example, to dollars*

1 *Look for £60 on the horizontal axis.*

2 *Read vertically upwards until you meet the line.*

3 *At the meeting point read horizontally across to the vertical axis.*

4 *Read the position of this point on the scale ($98).*

Use your head

Use the graph to convert

• £40 and £90 to dollars.

• $50 and $80 to pounds.

Averages

An **average** is one number chosen to represent a set of numbers.

It is a number somewhere near the middle of the set of numbers.

There are different types of average:

- The **mode** is the number which occurs most often.
- The **median** is the middle number when they are all put in order.
- The **mean** is the total of all the numbers divided by how many there are.

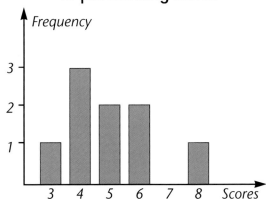

◀ *John had 9 turns at knocking down the pins. The numbers he knocked down each time were:*

4   3   4   5   6   4   5   8   6

10-pin bowling scores

▶ *A bar graph showing the scores looks like this:*

From the graph, the most frequent score is 4. The mode is 4.

To find the median, the scores are written in order:

3   4   4   4   <u>5</u>   5   6   6   8

The middle number is 5. The median is 5.

To find the mean, add the scores together:

$3 + 4 + 4 + 4 + 5 + 5 + 6 + 6 + 8 = 45$.

There are 9 numbers, so $45 \div 9 = 5$. The mean is 5.

All these different averages are near the middle of the set of numbers.

Look at the names and the number of letters in each.

What do you think the average number of letters in the names is?

Sue (3)	Natalie (7)	Joshua (6)
Shaun (5)	Kim (3)	Elroy (5)
Dean (4)	Kelly (5)	Hamid (5)
James (5)	Lucy (4)	

3   3   4   4   5   <u>5</u>   5   5   5   6   7

Writing the number of letters in order, we can see that:

The mode is 5.

The median is 5.

To find the mean, first find the total of the 11 numbers

$3 + 3 + 4 + 4 + 5 + 5 + 5 + 5 + 5 + 6 + 7 = 52$

Then $52 \div 11$ is between 4 and 5.

So, the mean is between 4 and 5.

Fun to do

Collect a set of the names of your friends.

Record the number of letters in each name. Find the mean, median and mode. How do they compare with the results above?

Dice throwing

If a dice is thrown, there are six different possible **outcomes**:

Each score is equally likely. This means that when the dice is thrown, each score has the same **chance** of appearing.

We can **predict** that approximately 1 out of 6, which is 6 out of 36, of the throws will show each number.

A prediction is a guess using what we know and understand.

We predict that the results will look approximately like this:

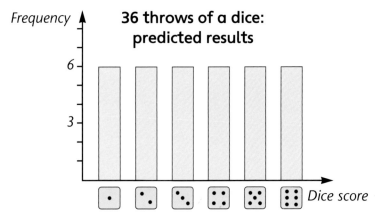

Now let's see what happens with a dice experiment.

A red dice is thrown 36 times.

These are the results shown in a **bar graph**:

Notice that what happens does not match exactly our predictions, but it is reasonably close.

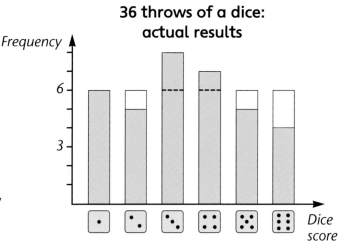

Fun to do

Throw your own dice 36 times, and see what happens, using the same predictions.

If two dice, one red and one green, are thrown
together, then there are 36 different possible outcomes.

If we throw them and find the total of the two dice,
then the answer can be any of 2 to 12.

The outcomes and totals are shown in an addition table:

+	1	2	3	4	5	6
1	2	3	4	5	6	7
2	3	4	5	6	7	8
3	4	5	6	7	8	9
4	5	6	7	8	9	10
5	6	7	8	9	10	11
6	7	8	9	10	11	12

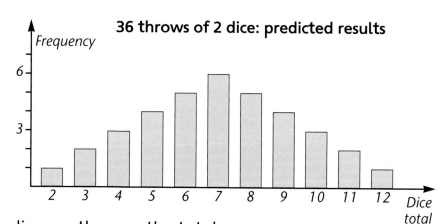

Notice that when the two dice are thrown, the totals
are not all equally likely. Some totals have more chance
of appearing than others. We can predict that the totals
will approximately match the bar graph.

Use your head

Which total has the greatest chance of appearing?
Which totals have the least chance?

Notice again,
that the results
are quite close to
our predictions.

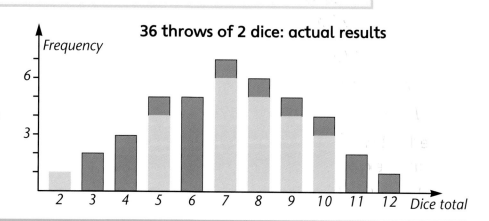

Fun to do

Throw your own red and green dice 36 times, and see
what happens to the totals, using the same predictions.

Glossary

average	a number we use to represent a typical or middle value in a set of numbers
axes/axis	graphs have two axes, the horizontal axis and the vertical axis
bar graph	graph which uses bars or columns to show information
bar-line graph	graph which uses straight lines to show amounts
block graph	graph which uses individual blocks which are joined to make columns to show information
chance	the chance of something happening is how likely it is to happen
conversion graph	line graph which is used to change or convert from one unit of measure to another
data	facts and information about something
database	large collection of data which can be sorted in different ways
distance table	table which helps you to find the distance between two places
frequency	the frequency of an event is the number of times it happens over a certain amount of time
frequency table	table showing different frequencies
graph	way of showing information as a picture to make it more easily understood
grouped frequency table	table showing different frequencies grouped together
horizontal line	straight line from left to right on paper which is held straight; a line parallel to the horizon
key	guide to explaining the meaning of a graph
line graph	graph which shows information by using lines to join up points

mean	an average which is found by dividing the total of a set of values by how many numbers there are
median	an average which is the middle value when a set is put in order from smallest to largest
mode	an average which is the most popular or frequent value in a set
outcome	a possible result of doing something
pictograph	graph which uses pictures to show data
pie chart	graph which shows data by cutting a circle (a pie) into slices of different sizes to show different amounts
predict	to guess based on what you know and understand
questionnaire	set of questions used to collect data
record sheet	sheet of paper used to write down collected data
spreadsheet	table of data, usually produced by a computer
statistics	the study of data
survey	finding information
tally mark	line or mark to score the number of times something occurs
tallying	method of counting
tally chart	chart or table for drawing tallies
Venn diagram	way of representing information using circles inside a rectangle
vertical line	straight line drawn from top to bottom, at right-angles to a horizontal line

Answers

Page 7
Use your head
vans: 7, bicycles: 17, cars: 22,
lorries: 11;
11; 14; 66

Page 8
Use your head
most often: vegetable,
least often: chicken;
3 tins; 11 tins

Page 9
Use your head
Sanjit: 8 slices, Katy: 5 slices,
Karen: 7 slices;
5 slices; 35 slices

Page 10
Use your head
11; 36; 49

Page 12
Question
6 red, 5 yellow, 4 blue, 3 green

Page 13
Use your head
7, 6, 9; 14, 15

Page 15
Use your head
Milan, Naples; one

Page 16
Use your head
Gary, Karen, Julie; Tiffany;
Sophie, Tiffany

Page 17
Use your head
Pat; Sharon; Greg; Pat; Dani; Tim

Page 19
Use your head
16: more than 10; 17: odd number
and more than 10; 18: more than
10 and multiple of 3; 19: odd
number and more than 10; 20:
more than 10

Page 20
Use your head
243 km, 417 km; Genoa and
Rome, Venice and Vienna

Page 21
Use your head
1-1; 2-0; 1-0

Page 23
Use your head
Dandy; Beezer and Whizzer

Page 24
Use your head
16.4°C, 19°C; 10:15

Page 25
Use your head
$64, $144; £31, £50

Page 29
Use your head
7; 2, 12

Index